THE GREATER CAUSE
STUDIES ON THE FAMILY FROM MATTHEW 19

STEVE PIXLER

THE GREATER CAUSE
STUDIES ON THE FAMILY FROM MATTHEW 19

STEVE PIXLER

Published by
Continuum Ministry Resources
5200 David Strickland Rd Fort Worth TX 76119

Published in the United States by
Continuum Ministry Resources
5200 David Strickland Rd.
Fort Worth, TX 76119

Printed in the United States of America

Cover design by Matt Brunson and Derrick Pulley

ISBN13: 978-0-9796261-0-4
ISBN10: 0-9796261-0-2

Library of Congress Cataloguing Information
2007930694

INTRODUCTION

Presumably, the introduction to a book is the best place for the author—that would be me—to tell his reading public—that would be you, both of you—what his book is about. However, I shall flummox tradition by presenting an introduction that begins by telling what this book is *not* about. It is *not* about divorce and remarriage. At least, it is not about divorce and remarriage strictly considered. Or even loosely considered, depending on your point of view. I have a wounded veteran's aversion to controversy on this topic, though I may overcome my native diffidence elsewhere later. That remains to be seen. I do appreciate the importance of such discussions, but for now I do not wish to cloud the larger issue addressed here.

And the larger issue addressed here—and this is where I pull my introduction back under the firm hand of tradition and tell you what this book is actually about—is the matter of strengthening Christian families by studying the principles of family life woven into the text of Jesus' remarks on divorce and remarriage in Matthew 19. We shall find these principles in every phrase of the Master's doctrine. Thus, if you thumb through this book looking for extended discussions on exception clauses and innocent parties, you will leave here sorely disappointed with nothing more than a smudge of ink on your thumb. However, if you peruse these few pages with a desire to learn from the Word of God how to build and preserve godly families, then I trust and pray that you will leave blessed by your perusal. The principles considered here are timeless and true. May God bless our efforts to learn, love and live them. Now, enough introduction already. Let's get started.

CHAPTER 1

Jesus' teaching on marriage and divorce in Matthew 19 begins with a backward glance at chapter eighteen. "And it came to pass, that when Jesus had finished these sayings...." Therefore, just before we get started on our study, we must pause for this profound observation: Matthew 19 follows Matthew 18. Now this should be obvious to even the meanest intelligence, as Wodehouse would say, but this point often escapes our notice. This means, then, that we should not proceed to Matthew 19 until we have looked over our shoulder to see what all the fuss was that brought about such a fierce controversy between Jesus and the local chapter of the Pharisees.

Matthew 18 begins with the disciples asking Jesus who should be the greatest in the kingdom of heaven. They were concerned with their rank and position in the coming kingdom. Jesus replied by setting a child in the midst of them and declaring that every believer must "be converted, and become as little children" to enter the kingdom. Salvation comes to those who are humble before God, not to those who seek to elevate themselves over others. Those who humble themselves are exalted. Further, those who receive children receive Christ Himself. Those who offend the little ones would be better off to leap into the sea adorned with a boulder necklace. This corrects the prevailing notion that human greatness is to be admired and weakness and vulnerability is to be despised. Jesus turns the world's pecking order on its head.

Jesus then spoke about "offenses," and He was not changing the subject. He was still speaking about the consequences of the disciples seeking "greatness," preeminence over one another. He warned against offending the "little ones," which occurs when those who consider themselves "great ones" despise their inferiors (as they suppose them). Jesus declared that He would gladly leave the ninety-nine sheep and seek after one lamb that is lost. It is not the will of God that even one of His little ones should be lost. Jesus taught these things to convert the minds of His disciples and show them that their worldly view of greatness and preeminence over others leads to division and offenses.

Jesus' example of the lost sheep was a smooth segue into a discussion of conflicts between brethren. Jesus insisted that believers work out their differences. Now, remember that all of this flows out the disciples' question concerning their positions in the kingdom. As Jesus showed, disputes between brethren cannot be settled when the parties involved are defending their "greatness." Humility is the fundamental basis for reconciliation and forgiveness. When men seek to assert their position and privilege, they cannot resolve disputes.

Apparently this bothered Peter a bit, prompting him to raise his hand and ask a question: "Lord, how oft shall my brother sin against me, and I forgive him? Till seven times?" Possibly Peter was thinking of one of the other disciples that irritated him early and often. Jesus replied, "I say not unto thee, until seven times: but, until seventy times seven." This must have been astounding. We have heard the words of Jesus for a lifetime and they no longer amaze. Indeed, we have heard the words of Christ so often that we generally tune them out. However, this was the first time the words were uttered and it must have caused quite a sensation. We are to forgive our brother four hundred and ninety times daily? That is quite unreasonable! This is the sort of outrageous preaching that cracked like a whip from the end of Jesus' tongue. And, as we shall see, Peter was not the only incredulous listener in the crowd that day.

And Jesus, rather than backing off from statements made while in the grip of a rash and impractical anointing, drove the point even further home by telling the story of the king who came to take account of his servants. As the story goes, the king forgave one servant a large debt. This forgiven servant promptly found another who owed him far less, and rather than imitating the good example of his merciful master, he seized his debtor by the throat and demanded that the lesser debt be paid immediately. When the unfortunate servant could not pay the minuscule debt, the thankless servant cast his fellow in prison until the debt could be paid. This outrage was brought to the master's attention, and he was infuriated by the ungrateful servant's behavior. He angrily revoked the original forgiveness and reinstated the debt. And thus, Jesus said, driving the point all the way home, shall our heavenly Father do to us if we do not forgive our brothers their trespasses.

So, chapter eighteen begins with the disciples striving with one another about who should be the greatest and asking Jesus to settle their rivalry by informing them in advance of their future positions and ranking in the kingdom of heaven. Jesus sighed in frustration and launched into a powerful message on the dangers of seeking greatness and the blessings of serving others in true humility. Jesus then rebuked them for despising the weak and defenseless, the "little ones," and taught them how to work out their differences through forgiveness and restoration. This theme of humility and forgiveness flows in an unbroken current throughout chapter eighteen. And, soon enough, this stream carries us directly into the open waters of chapter nineteen and the heated discussion on divorce.

This arrangement of material in Matthew's gospel is obviously providential. Jesus' teaching on divorce in the Sermon on the Mount (Matthew 5) follows the same pattern. Jesus spoke concerning settling disputes and then launched directly into His doctrine on marriage. There must be something here connecting forgiveness and marriage that we need to consider.

Indeed, we may as well begin right here applying the Word to the problem of family renewal. That is what we have come to this passage to do. Problems in the family arise from the same sin from which problems in the church arise: pride. This sort of division is the result of proud rivalries over "who shall be the greatest." Conflicts flow out of contention over who gets their way. "Only by pride cometh contention" (Proverbs 13:10). All that is necessary for spectacular conflict is more than one proud person dwelling in the same space long enough. Offenses shall come.

Sin first entered the human race when Adam sought to attain greatness—to be "like God knowing good and evil"—through this sort of proud self-promotion. The quest for prominence and jockeying for position leads to rivalries between husbands and wives, parents and children, brothers and sisters and so on. The only remedy for such familial conflict is what Jesus taught His disciples: humility and forgiveness. We must seek to occupy the familial office we have been given (for distinct offices have been given) with genuine humility, and we must carefully and quickly settle disputes in the manner Jesus taught, forgiving one another with determined resolve.

Paul discussed humility and forgiveness in close context with marriage relations in at least two places (Ephesians 4-5 and Colossians 3). Paul spoke at length about the mind of Christ in Philippians 2 and insisted that Christians must be like Christ, which, of course, is what the word "Christian" means. So, those who want a Christian home must *be* Christians at home. We must humble ourselves and put on the mind of Christ. We must be "kind one to another, tenderhearted, forgiving one another even as God for Christ's hath forgiven [us]" (Ephesians 4:32). Understanding Jesus' doctrine on humility and forgiveness in Matthew 18 is fundamental to understanding His teaching on Christian marriage in Matthew 19.

On now into chapter 19. When Jesus wrapped up His teaching, He "departed from Galilee, and came into the coasts of Judea beyond Jordan; and great multitudes followed him; and he healed them there." Possibly this move could represent for us a decision to forsake the land of offense and conflict and enter into a land of healing and restoration. Certainly those who seek healing for their family must make this sort of move.

As long as we live in the land where the seeds of offense are carefully cultivated into full-grown grudges we shall eat of the bitter harvest of hateful spite. And the multitudes "followed Him; and He healed them there." Those who were willing to leave the land of offense and conflict, those who were willing to forsake their proud prerogatives of power and position (alliteration alert!) and seek humble restoration, found the healing for which they had long prayed.

Jesus' teaching always attracts needy people. And there is no area of life where we are needier than in our families. This is why those who desperately long for family renewal are turning back to the teaching of the Lord for answers. We are tired of pop-psychology and the empty promises of secular humanism. We need healing, and thus we seek the Healer. But if we seek the Healer, we must get up and get out of the bitter land. We must take up our cross and follow Him to a land of restoration. Family healing requires family discipleship. The principles of the doctrine of Christ bring deliverance, but not apart from faithful discipleship. Those who misappropriate the principles of Christ as mere tactics for self-improvement inevitably distort grace into law and by sowing after the flesh reap corruption. We must follow Him to be healed.

CHAPTER 2

The news of Jesus' radical teaching on forgiveness must have made the wires fairly quickly. The religious elites in Jerusalem soon caught wind of the hubbub and came to hear it for themselves. As the crowds were gathered around Jesus to be healed a small group of Pharisees swollen with self-importance pushed their way to the front of the line. They had a question to ask. They had thought of several situations where all this nonsense about humility and forgiveness simply could not apply. Marriage and divorce, for example. No one could expect a man to be so forgiving to his wife. It simply isn't done. The man's power and prestige in the home would be gravely threatened if he afforded such consideration to the female. That sort of thing could get out of hand.

It is fairly amazing how quickly Jesus' teaching flushed the Pharisees out. Jesus' teaching about disputes between brethren must have started them thinking about quarrels at home. They even may have recalled a divorce or two lurking in their past when they invoked their privilege and power as husband to cast the little wife out with nothing but a bill of divorcement in her hand. All legal and proper, you understand, but not a great deal of forgiveness in it. All that talk about offending little ones must have rankled.

It is almost impossible for a man to hear preaching about quarrels and division without his mind finding its way back home. There is no subject nearer to a man than his family. And every man knows whether or not he has been all the man he should be in the privacy of his home. A man may keep up the public charade of kindness and consideration, but he knows that his family knows. It is impossible to hide the truth from those who share shelter with us every day. Jesus' incisive teaching struck home, quite literally.

So the Pharisees came. The hypocrites always do. Wherever there is a crowd of sincere, needy people praying for healing and restoration, the hypocrites always come along. But they do not come for help. They come for self-justification, and that's a different thing altogether. As Matthew says, "The Pharisees also came unto him, tempting him." They came to tempt Jesus, to put Him to the test. They came to prove that His doctrine of forgiveness and humility was weak and impractical. Looks good on paper, Jesus, but it does not work out in real life. They came to prove that there are some instances where a man must take a stand and refuse to forgive. They came to defend the right of hard-hearted men to summarily throw their wives out at the slightest provocation.

This just goes to show that we learn who a man really is when he is at home. His public persona is generally a mask worn to project a carefully cultivated image. This is why Paul was so insistent that the true measure of a man's qualification for ministry is his home life (1 Timothy 3:4). Watch how a man continually treats his wife and children and you will see the heart of that man truly revealed.

The Pharisees proposed the question they had so carefully prepared: "Is it lawful for a man to put away his wife for every cause?" They came tempting Him. They were not looking for truth; they were looking for loopholes. They were legalists. They were seeking to justify their unforgiving hearts with select Scriptures carefully finessed. This is the danger that all hardhearted men (and women) face when they begin surveying their grounds for divorce. It is almost impossible to pursue divorce as a resolution to marital strife without becoming a self-justifying legalist. Who ever heard of a man or woman entering divorce court and approaching the bench loudly proclaiming personal responsibility for their share of the problem? "Judge, let the record show that this break-up is entirely my fault!" Not hardly. People with that approach never make it to divorce court. They end up at the altar renewing vows and celebrating golden anniversaries. Those in divorce court go there pointing fingers and casting blame. Anything less adversely affects custody battles and alimony settlements.

Neither husband nor wife is ever completely innocent in a divorce. Both the man and the woman share in the blame for the demise of a marriage. They may not share in the blame equally, but they share it nonetheless. However, our approach to the issue often mirrors the Pharisees. We come waving the letter of the law and pleading our case, pointing fingers and explaining why and how we were right all the way through. As a pastor, I can never remember a time when a couple came into my office for marital counseling that I did not spend the first few minutes listening to each one explain why everything (mostly) was the other's fault. The first sign of progress comes when the man and then the woman begin to see where they could have done things differently and begin to accept responsibility for their share of the problem. This is why I say that both parties to a divorce share the blame. The Pharisees would have been wiser men if they had whipped out their copies of the law to find where they could have done better. The Word is supposed to be a mirror, not a magnifying glass. Certainly there are times that divorce may be unavoidable, but we must be careful that we do not imitate the proud approach of the Pharisees.

The Pharisees asked Jesus if He considered it lawful for a man to divorce his wife "for every cause." There is no list here offering samples of what their pet causes may have been, and modern speculation runs from burning the biscuits to moral turpitude. However, the Pharisees had no wish to narrow it down that much, anyway. They were making a larger point about the man's right to cast out his wife according to his own whim. They wanted to show that conflict resolution is not always possible, *contra* Jesus' teaching.

I understand, of course, that there were larger theological issues at stake. Ancient debates raged among the rabbis concerning divorce. Hillel and Shammai (via their students) had fussed for years about all of this. But the Pharisees were not requesting Jesus to settle long standing feuds between certain rabbinic schools. They were *tempting* Jesus. They were trying to trap Him into an admission of the inadequacy of His own doctrine. And they failed rather largely.

However, the main thing that I wish to emphasize here is the fact that the Pharisees presented divorce as being a result of certain causes. And, oddly enough, they were right on the money in this one thing. Divorce always does have a cause. Divorce does not occur as an unexplained natural phenomenon. Most folks know why they busted up. Divorce, we might say, is a matter of cause and effect. Burned biscuits are the cause, and divorce is the effect, with a lot of fussing and fighting in-between, buttering the charred remains.

This is very important to our study of the greater cause. We must gasp this idea right here that divorce is a matter of cause and effect. *Something* causes the fracturing of the home. Every divorce can be traced back to a root cause. A seed of offense is planted and becomes a root of bitterness. The offense grows daily until it becomes a giant tree of thorns that swallows up the verdant garden of the home and casts its bitter fruit in every room. The encroaching roots of bitterness break up the foundation of the home until, finally, the tree topples like the hollow oak over the decaying structure of a once happy home. And it all happened just *because.* Mighty oaks from little acorns grow.

Everyone who goes through a divorce has their own list of causes. Ask them what happened and they will gladly fill you in. During legal proceedings, the judge will always inquire of attorneys as they represent the demise of a marriage: "What are the grounds for divorce?" The grounds vary. Some will allege cruelty, others infidelity. And these are truly awful grounds for divorce, if true. However, these days most folks merely offer "irreconcilable differences" as the grounds for divorce. They just cannot get along, it seems. Or, they may even seek a "no fault" divorce, missing the irony altogether.

However, here is the bottom line: every divorce is the proud promotion of someone's selfish cause. Humility and forgiveness do not play well in this arena. The man who puts away his wife must contend that his cause for divorce is greater than his cause for staying together and working it out. It is a conflict of causes, and the cause for giving up is greater than the cause for trying again. That is the theme that I shall pound like a nail throughout our study.

CHAPTER 3

So—the Pharisees had sprung their big question. They waited with bated breath to see if Jesus would stumble into their well-laid trap. He did not. Moreover, Jesus wasted no time preparing a careful response. He had a ready answer for them. Jesus always does have answers, for as one man sang Jesus *is* the answer. And yet He immediately put His finger on the Pharisees' problem: "Have ye not read?" Well, of course, they had read the forthcoming reference, but they had not *read* it. They had read the letter of the law—probably had committed it to memory—but they missed the Spirit of it altogether. They were legalistic, "someone-help-me-find-a-loophole" readers, not sincere "help-me-see-where-I-am-wrong" readers.

Jesus is still putting His finger on the problem today. The Spirit still speaks expressly that our only remedy for our marriage and family problems is the Word of God. We must *read* when we read. We must go beneath the surface of the text and implore the Holy Spirit to reveal Christ to us through the Word that we may behold Him there and be transformed into His image and glory. The answer is not found in pop-psychology and humanistic self-help. The answer is still found in the words of God.

Jesus drew the Pharisees' attention to what they had missed. First of all, they missed that "He which made them at the beginning made them male and female." *God* made them; He made them *at the beginning*; and He made them *male and female*. In this one statement Jesus highlighted three profound truths. First, the man and the woman and the marriage that united them were all created by God. Marriage is not a human institution. This means that our ideas on marriage must be formed by the law of God not the whim of man. Second, marriage is a creation ordinance, and thus we must look all the way back to the beginning to truly understand its original form and function. Paul also considered marriage as a creation ordinance in his discussion on headship in I Corinthians 11.

We must dwell on the third point for just a moment. God made them *male and female*. This is another one of those profound truths that is so obvious that it is routinely overlooked. God made them *male and female*. In other words, God is not surprised that men and women are different. He deliberately made them so. He put Adam to sleep and drew a profoundly different creature out of his side. The woman came from the man and is flesh of his flesh and bone of his bones, but the similarities end there. Again: that should be obvious even to a casual observer; men and women are different. And yet, modern intellectuals often need government funded research studies to establish the fact.

However, the point to be made here is that God created marriage to be the joint effort of two very different people, the harmonizing of two separate notes. This is how good music is made, and love songs are no exception. God declared that it was not good for man to be alone, so He gave him a helpmeet. God was not merely observing sympathetically that the poor man needed company, someone to stave off loneliness in the midnight hour. Certainly companionship is a wonderful part of marriage, but it is only a part. When God said that it was not good for man to be alone, He meant that it is not good for a man to live by and for himself. Man needs to live for a purpose beyond his own self-interest. May I say it now? Man needs a *greater cause*.

God pulled out of man a complementary (not compl*i*mentary, though that also helps sometimes) creature that would balance man's self-centered orientation toward the world. God gave the man a dance partner. God never intended for the man to hog the spotlight and groove his way across the dance floor alone, John Travolta notwithstanding. That sort of thing is never pretty no matter how many attempt it. The entire universe is created to move in rhythm with its Maker, and God created the man and woman to mirror this cosmic pirouette. In other words, God deliberately gave the man a woman that was his opposite. He made them male and female.

Now this is important. It is right here that the troubles begin. Soon after they are married, if not before, the man starts acting like a man and the woman like a woman, and all Hades breaks loose. Someone said that women are from Venus and men are from Mars, though I have not heard how they purport to know. Something to do with NASA and the Hubble Telescope, I suppose. Really, I do not have a clue exactly what that means, but quite possibly it is another way of saying that men and women are different. If so, then I concur. These space travelers may be on to something.

But as I said: the troubles begin when the man starts acting like a man and the woman starts acting like a woman. Each surprises the other with this alien behavior, and mild and loving recriminations ensue. At first. Then love's warm glow begins to fade, however, when the parties to the marriage keep on acting like *other*. The man gets frustrated because the woman behaves in an irrational and emotional way (to preserve a generally accurate stereotype), and the woman gets frustrated because he is coldly logical and always wants to fix problems that she just wants to talk about (to go on preserving a generally accurate stereotype). She *feels,* and he *thinks,* and both begin to view the other with frank concern. Something is wrong with *them*—they are not like *me.*

The man gets frustrated and is tempted to tell the little woman to just buck up and be a man. And yet—hold it!—that does not work. No man, at least no man who is truly a man, wants to marry another man. (That is a problem we have not the space to address. Another time and place, possibly.) The woman seeks out female companionship and shares her sorrows with someone who will cluck sympathetically without trying to fix anything. The man just goes fishing. They are facing the age-old difficulty of synchronizing the orbit of two radically different worlds.

This does not mean that marriage should be a constant clash of wills. Indeed, the great challenge of marriage is to properly align disparate wills. But this cannot be done simply by the dominant will obliterating the lesser one, somewhat like a Martian-Venusian War of the Worlds. Jesus commanded those who aspire to greatness not to despise the weakness of the little ones. Peter commanded the man to "[give] honor unto the wife as unto the weaker vessel…that your prayers be not hindered" (I Peter 3:7), though we must also note in passing (and that very quickly) that certainly there are occasions when the feminine will is the dominant one. There must be a genuine harmonizing of the masculine and feminine will, which can only be done as both man and the woman submit to a will higher than their own. May I say it again? They must submit to a greater cause.

This is certainly how it works. Any couple married for any length of time can see their portrait painted here in print. And yet, this is how it is *supposed* to work. God created the world as a place of diversity and beauty through contrast. This is what is so deeply ironic about sexually maladjusted moderns who confuse diversity with homogeneity. They contend that homosexuality is a celebration of diversity, plastering rainbows on every flat surface as a radiant symbol of their folly. But homosexuality is best symbolized in monochrome black bars depicting the enslavement of their depressing uniformity. That sort of flat, perverse sameness is anything but gay. It is not good for man to be alone. And yet, this is what they do when they seek *same* (homosexual) rather than *other* (heterosexual). They miss out on the beauty of life when it is lived in the delirious rhythms of a dance with *other*.

Opposites attract. It takes both a negative and a positive for a spark, a charge and a current. No wonder the world is run down. They are missing out on the electrifying power of true diversity, the diversity of a man loving his wife as Christ loves the church. Now, Christian men have to pay close attention right here. Though most men quickly repudiate actual homosexuality, it is entirely possible to impose a sort of "virtual homosexuality" on the marriage by refusing to embrace the otherness of the other. Many men expect their wife to be their shadow, a *sotto voce* echo of their brash masculine voice, and so create a weird sort of same-sex marriage.

Relationship is an expression of love, and love requires an object. It is not good for man to be alone, for then man's love is self-referential. This sort of love ends up as raw narcissism. Paul taught that men are born loving themselves, but man's subjective self-love must mature into objective, self-denying love for others. No one has to teach a little boy how to love his own flesh. And this is not necessarily a sin at first. But he must grow out of this self-love into the love of another. His sexual development is an apt physical metaphor and genuine embodiment of this spiritual reality. It is not good for a man to be alone. Of course, this sort of sacrificial love is the love of God, the love that God has manifest from eternity toward Christ and the church, and fallen man cannot know this love without first knowing the love of God. We love God because He first loved us, and this reciprocal love overflows in boundless waves into the lives of others. Love like this is built into the very physiological, biological make-up of men and women. God made it so when He made them male and female.

This is where the true challenge, the wondrous adventure of relationship, lies. We must learn to love to learn to live. This is why we pity the homosexual who will never know the joy of living and loving. It is also why we should pity the man who sleeps with a woman every night without ever allowing her to truly be the woman God created her to be. You know the type. He is proud of the fact that his home, his food, his cars, his money—his everything—is just the way *he* likes it, and no woman is going to spoil his bachelor pad with so much as a whiff of femininity. It *really* is not good for a man to be alone.

This man is not man enough to allow his wife to be a woman. He is every bit as enamored with himself as is the man who makes love to himself, or to his closest counterpart, another man. He is a virtual homosexual. He simply does not act it out sexually. Furthermore, probably the deepest irony of self-love is that it ultimately becomes self-loathing if it is not transformed by the love of God into love for others. And then we are confronted with the weirdest sort of hybrid emotion, the love-hate relationship of a terminally egocentric man who hates the self he worships. That fellow will be hard to live with. Just ask his partner.

CHAPTER 4

God made Adam and Eve male and female at the beginning and said (through Adam), "For this cause shall a man leave father and mother, and shall cleave to his wife: and they twain shall be one flesh." This is where Jesus' response starts getting real interesting. The Pharisees opened the volley with a question about divorce "for every cause." Jesus returned the serve with a very powerful "for this cause." Jesus quite deliberately set up a pointed conflict between the "for every cause" of the Pharisees and the "for this cause" of the Creator. It is a conflict of causes, man's cause versus God's cause, and only one cause can win.

God created marriage for a purpose. And God's purpose must always remain paramount. This is what the Pharisees, in their haste to justify themselves and ensnare Jesus in His own doctrine, overlooked completely. They could only think of their own causes for divorce. However, there is a greater cause. God created marriage to facilitate man's dominion over all creation. Man was created in the image and likeness of God and given dominion over everything God had made. Indeed, dominion is an expression of the image of God. God is King over all the earth, and Adam mirrored that reality. Adam was crowned as regent prince over the fowls of the air, the beasts of the field and the fish of the sea. However, God soon made it plain that He did not expect man to accomplish this rule alone. So, God gave man a helpmeet, a fitting helper to assist him in the task of dominion. Further, God gave Adam and his wife the promise of many children to perpetuate and propagate the purpose of God in the earth. Marriage and childbearing were given to man for the purpose of universal dominion. Thus, if I may jump ahead of myself just a bit, a man can either pursue dominion or sue for divorce; he cannot do both.

From the very beginning, therefore, the purpose of God is directly tied up with the human family. God could have done things differently if He had so chosen, but He did not. He ordained that His glory would extend from sea to sea through the agency of the human family. God told Adam, "Be fruitful, and multiply, and replenish the earth, and subdue it: and have dominion." There is no dominion, no replenishing the earth and subduing it without the "be fruitful and multiply." The means of dominion is the family. God made it so. The Lord God repeated this creation mandate to Noah, Abraham, Isaac, Jacob and the people of Israel. Throughout Scripture it becomes evident that God intends to subdue the earth through the instrumentality of the human family. Psalm 127 is a wonderful example of the role of the family in the task of dominion. Our children are God's arrows of war sent out into the earth for the victory of the kingdom.

Furthermore, this approach does not change in the New Testament. That may fly in the face of popular opinion, but popular opinion is wrong. God still intends to use the family as the means of dominion. The gospel may divide the family at times, but this is not intended to be the permanent condition of the faithful home. New households must be built and godly dynasties established, and this sometimes causes division in the old, unbelieving order. But once the new household of faith is established, we should expect God to rear up the entire family and ensuing generations in persevering faithfulness. Peter understood this when he boldly proclaimed that the gospel is preached and the promise of salvation is offered to the entire family: "For the promise is unto and to your *children*" (Acts 2:39).

Many other examples can be found in the New Testament where household salvation was the norm and not the exception. Paul taught believers that their faith sanctifies their spouse and children and provides them the hope of full salvation (I Corinthians 7). The unbeliever is not saved merely by being married to a believer, but he certainly has a head start. Peter echoed the same promise when he assured the godly wife that her chaste lifestyle could win her disobedient husband to the faith (I Peter 3). The family is still God's means of evangelizing the world and gaining dominion in every nation. Celibate service is the exception not the rule (I Corinthians 7). The early church evangelized Jerusalem from house to house. This was not an ancient form of door-to-door canvassing (though that has its place). Rather it was household evangelism where the gospel was preached from family to family. The bottom line is this: God created marriage and family to be the means of multiplying His dominion over all the earth. Divorce frustrates that grand design.

This is why God hates divorce. He *hates* it. It does not matter that there may be instances where divorce is unavoidable, and it does not matter that even God Himself permitted and regulated its practice (as we shall discuss below). God still hates divorce. Period. There is *no* time that God likes it. It is *always* a frustration of His purpose and plan for mankind.

The Lord put it rather bluntly in Malachi 2:

> Yet ye say, Wherefore? Because the LORD hath been witness between thee and the wife of thy youth, against whom thou hast dealt treacherously: yet is she thy companion, and the wife of thy covenant. And did not he make one? Yet had he the residue of the spirit. And wherefore one? That he might seek a godly seed. Therefore take heed to your spirit, and let none deal treacherously against the wife of his youth. For the LORD, the God of Israel, saith that he hateth putting away: for one covereth violence with his garment, saith the LORD of hosts: therefore take heed to your spirit, that ye deal not treacherously. Ye have wearied the LORD with your words. Yet ye say, Wherein have we wearied him? When ye say, Every one that doeth evil is good in the sight of the

LORD, and he delighteth in them; or, Where is the God of judgment? (Malachi 2:14-17)

That makes the matter rather clear. God hates divorce. No two ways about it. But notice why God hates divorce: "And did not he make one? Yet had he the residue of the spirit. And wherefore one? That he might seek a godly seed." God made man and woman one flesh so that "He might seek a godly seed." He could have created a hundred Adams with twice as many Eves. But He chose one man and one woman that He might obtain a godly seed. The seed was ultimately Christ Himself, but God determined to preserve an elect family lineage to provide a direct line through which Christ would come. The elect family provided a safe house for the seed to grow. Salvation was never automatic to members of the elect family; salvation has always been by grace through faith in both the Old and New Covenants. The New Testament argues this point extensively. Neither was salvation limited exclusively to the godly lineage; there are numerous examples of God-fearing Gentiles outside of Israel. However, God's purpose was inextricably bound up with the chosen seed. The preservation of the seed was God's highest priority. Divorce and family disintegration frustrated this priority.

The Lord established the godly lineage when He commanded Adam and Eve to be fruitful and multiply. After Adam sinned, God did not revoke His creation mandate to be fruitful and multiply. His plan still required the godly seed, and the Lord foretold the great struggle between the seed of the woman and the seed of the serpent, a struggle that was played out ultimately at Calvary in Christ and continues today through the church. Noah's Flood was God's judgment upon the earth to prevent the total loss of the seed through genealogical confusion. All through the Old Testament there were constant struggles by Satan to destroy the seed of the righteous and miraculous interventions by God to preserve them. This is the heart of Old Testament history. It is all about the Saga of the Seed.

Divorce divides the home and wastes the godly seed. Satan seems to have learned somewhere that a house divided against itself cannot stand. He has also picked up the idea that you cannot spoil a strong man's house until you first bind the strongman. The family is falling and the children are the spoils of war due to the tragic rise of divorce among believers. This trend must be reversed. We must recognize divorce for the danger that it is. Satan greatest weapon against the godly seed is divorce.

God created marriage to be a lifelong relationship between one man and woman so that they might rear up enduring generations of the godly seed. We must submit all of our reasons for breaking up to God's great reason for staying together. We must learn to work our problems out so God may work His purpose in us. God's purpose must come first. Marriage was created to perpetuate a faithful people unto God. Divorce frustrates that purpose. Marriage was created for God's cause. Divorce is created for man's cause. Which cause is greater?

CHAPTER 5

This means that we must radically reorient our way of thinking about marriage and its purpose. Our world's view of marriage is very self-centered. We mainly view marriage as the means of satisfying our inherent desire for romance, relationship, both spousal and parental, and economic stability. Marriage is generally pursued to satisfy our emotional and physical needs and to make us happy. Indeed, the climactic phrase of any fairy tale love story is, "And they lived happily ever after." When marriage is viewed from this perspective happiness is the greater cause. Thus, when the marriage is no longer producing happiness, it is time to end the marriage. Divorce seems the quickest way to restore immediate happiness. Of course, anyone who actually has ever been through a divorce knows that this is a joke. Things will never be the same again—*ever*. A divorce never really ends a relationship, particularly if there are children involved. It is like trying to pull two pieces of paper apart that have been glued together with super glue. You may get the papers apart, but not without tearing them both. Divorce does not restore everyone back to their original condition, and it does not restore happiness.

Happiness is attained when it is not the goal. Possibly the pursuit of happiness is a God-given right, but that is not the way to reach it. It is somewhat like shouting angrily at a party of bickering children, "You *will* have fun!" You cannot force people to have fun, and you cannot force happiness into a relationship. Happiness comes when men and women learn to live for things greater than their own personal satisfaction. Happiness comes from outside us. It comes from having a larger purpose and meaning in life than just being happy. This is why Jesus' teaching is so incisive and helpful. The Pharisees were betraying the fundamental problem that complicates relationships and makes divorce an option in the first place. Marriages are falling apart because they are built on the sandy foundation of personal happiness rather than on the solid rock of God's eternal purpose. And the ultimate irony is that when we stop seeking happiness and start seeking God's everlasting purpose for our home we find happiness. As Jesus said elsewhere, if we lose our life we shall find it.

Our flawed perspective on marriage begins during childhood. This is especially true in American culture where childishness, going about under the alias "individualism," is perpetuated throughout our lifetimes as the mark of truly meaningful existence. Immaturity—i.e., selfishness—has been acculturated and institutionalized. We are born selfish, but we are supposed to grow out of it. We should be growing up, which means growing beyond self. The individual is created to find its fulfillment a part of a larger whole. However, our approach to marriage brings this childish perspective all the way down the center aisle to the wedding altar. We are conditioned to believe that marriage will be the fulfillment of all of our personal hopes and dreams. We never stop to ask if there is a deeper meaning.

The first question that should be asked of a young couple considering marriage is, "Why do you want to get married?" Most couples would respond that they want to get married because they love one another. But love is no reason to get married—at least not the sort of love that the world promotes. The love of the world is totally different from biblical love. Biblical love is defined as laying down your life for the good of another. Jesus said, "Greater love hath no man than this, that a man lay down his life for his friends" (John 15:13). That is what true love is, the willingness to die for another. The world's love is not that sort of love at all. The world's love is mere affection. It is romantic desire for another because the other satisfies an emotional need within self. The world's love is a self-centered love that seeks its own satisfaction, not the well-being of another. This is *lust*, not love. So the young couple would probably be more honest if they answered why they want to get married with, "We lust for one another." Of course, that sort of honesty might delay the proceedings just a bit.

This selfish approach to marriage is inculcated by our process of spouse selection, an insane rite of passage we call "dating." We call it dating because the boy and girl set a date to spend time alone together, ostensibly to learn the ropes of male-female relationships and find their soul-mate. What they really learn is that they must engage in repeated-random-remote-recreational-romance until they find someone who makes them happy, selfishly defined. They are led on a mad quest to satisfy the dictates of their heart. Indeed, their heart becomes their principal guide and counselor. "But, daddy, I *love* him!" she says. These impressionable and foolish children forget that their "heart is deceitful above all things, and desperately wicked: who can know it?" (Jeremiah 17:9). But they have been taught from a child to trust their hearts and forget all other considerations. And now those children are getting married.

Love (read: "lust") has been successfully enthroned as the god of our age. But this love is really nothing other than self-love projected onto an adored object. Let the loved one fail to make the lover happy and you will see how quickly love can be turned to hate. One fellow compared this sort of selfish love to the love a boy has for ice cream. He does not really love the ice cream: he loves the sensation that ice cream gives to him. This is not true love, not in the biblical sense.

Never in the history of the world has a culture prepared its children for adult relationships in such a foolish and cavalier way. Preparation for marriage had always been a family affair with the authority of the bride's father firmly in place and holding back the unwelcome advances of unsuitable suitors until sophisticated moderns dismissed the traditional approach as out of touch with more enlightened sensibilities. Now, our feckless fathers turn out their young girls into the night to be an easy prey for rabid brutes prowling high on testosterone. At the doorstep, as he sees his darling off into the night with another recent acquaintance, dad feels a momentary flicker of silent concern that she does not bring home the inconvenient annoyance of pregnancy. That will not do. That sort of thing might interrupt the game, or maybe even force him to turn off the TV altogether. He can only hope for the best. And this is what passes for enlightened modern parenting. We must let the children follow their hearts. The truth is this *faux* enlightenment is introducing a new dark age where we are now facing the total collapse of family, society and culture, in that order.

Dating is divorce practice. It teaches our children to give their heart away and then take it back as many times as necessary to find happiness. If Bill does not make her happy, then she will try Joe. If Joe fails, try Jim. On and on until she finds one that deceives her long enough to get married. And then, lo and behold, this one proves to be a man just like all the rest, sorry rascal, and she realizes that marriage is just not making her nearly as happy as she dreamed it would. So, divorce becomes an option. Then, as she broods on her misery, it becomes a necessity. She must do whatever it takes to recover her happiness. She knows this because she learned it at her mommy's knee.

It is time to reject this folly and return to biblical principles of preparing for marriage. We must radically revolutionize our approach to marriage and teach our children daily that marriage was created by God for a larger purpose than our own personal happiness. We must teach them that real happiness is found in seeking something greater than happiness. We must demonstrate before our children that marriage is simply a new and different phase of serving the Lord for a lifetime. We must proclaim the creation mandate, to be fruitful and multiply, to replenish the earth and have dominion over it. They must see marriage as a team effort at doing the will of God. When marriage is viewed this way, then God's cause becomes the greater cause, and every dispute can be addressed and resolved in light of the family's commitment to the greater cause. We must work this out in true humility and forgiveness in order to do the will of God. That is the greater cause.

This is a completely different way of looking at marriage and divorce. The Pharisees must have been taken aback. They were not expecting this. Surely they realized that Jesus had a point. Divorce frustrates the purpose of God. And true believers should always seek to elevate the purpose of God over their own purposes for life. Every Christian that sincerely submits his life to the teaching of Jesus is confronted by this same reality. God created marriage for His purpose, the purpose of growing the kingdom of God in the earth through the propagation of godly seed. It is impossible to pursue divorce without frustrating this purpose. Again, though divorce is sometimes unavoidable, it is always undesirable.

CHAPTER 6

G od made them male and female for the purpose of subduing the earth and bringing glory to Him forever. God created the family as the vehicle for this task. God's method has not changed. He still intends to use the family, the godly seed, as the means of fulfilling His eternal purpose. This is the reason for marriage, and thus, it is the reason men get married. At least, this is supposed to be the reason that men get married. It seems that a few other reasons have crept in along the way. Many men go into the world to make their mark, to make their fortune, or to seek after pleasure. Count the reasons; they are manifold. But from the beginning it was not so. From the beginning God intended that, "For this cause shall a man leave father and mother, and shall cleave to his wife: and they twain shall be one flesh." The man should leave home to build a home. All other pursuits should flow out of this purpose. Men should seek education, vocation, fortune, pleasure, on and on, for the purpose of building a godly house. Man was made to be a family man.

There are instances when men are called to celibate service, but, as noted above, this is the rare exception. Furthermore, most modern men who reject the married life are not doing out of any noble desire for the celibate life. Most reject marriage because they want the "freedom" to play the field and be a child in a man's body. They have lived just long enough to throw off all restraint and indulge every selfish whim. (These men are really whimmin.) They have forgotten the words of the apostle, "When I was a child, I spake as a child, I understood as a child, I thought as a child: but when I became a man, I put away childish things" (I Corinthians 13:11). They have not grown up; they have just grown taller.

The natural order of things is for a man to leave home to embark on his vocation, build a house, take a wife, father children and extend the rule and reign of man over the earth under the authority of Christ. Dominion is man's destiny. Man was created to rule the world. However the prodigal sons of our dissolute culture cannot rule themselves much less their world. They have no dominion over their own spirit so they cannot take dominion over the earth. How can a man subdue the earth and cultivate it as a worldwide Garden of Eden when he is busy sowing his wild oats? And then he wakes up in the hog pen with only a faint memory of how a godly household really functions. We have taught our men to wait on marriage as long as possible and enjoy the single life as the ultimate expression of personal freedom. They are like the wild ass of the wilderness that "snuffeth up the wind." But God said that men should leave father and mother "for this cause" of marriage. No doubt the world values every other selfish cause as greater than settling down and rearing a family, but the world is wrong. God's cause is still the greater cause.

"For this cause shall a man *leave* father and mother, and shall *cleave* to his wife" (emphasis added). The words of God here indicate something more formal than just Junior leaving home as soon as possible when he turns eighteen. The "leaving" refers to a covenantal rite of passage when the father and mother send their son out into the world—they *commission* him, if you will—to extend the reach of the godly family. The father and mother lay their hands upon the son, call him by name and bless him. They give him the inheritance that belongs to him and help him get his feet on the ground as he lays the foundation of a new Christian household. His household will be a separate, sovereign house, but dad and mom remain involved. They are committed to helping their son be successful as a husband and father. They do not control his home, for he is "leaving" father and mother and "cleaving" to his wife. But they do remain available for godly counsel and direction. He is the man of the new house, and as a wise man he draws from the well of his parent's Christian experience.

This is altogether the message of the Proverbs, which is actually written by parents to prepare their son for life as an adult.

The "cleaving" refers to the covenantal union that is formed when a man and woman marry. The word translated "cleave" in Genesis 3 has a broad range of meaning that includes "to pursue," "to take" and "to hold fast." If I can run these meanings together, to cleave to a wife means to pursue, take and embrace a wife. This indicates that the man must take the initiative in pursuing marriage, which is the way the human race has generally behaved until, happily, modern intellectuals arrived on the stage of world history just in time to show us where millennia of human history has been wrong. Leaving and cleaving also means that the man must follow (pursue) the proper protocol of courting a woman and requesting her hand in marriage. Unless, of course, we choose to imitate the world's great wisdom in turning out our daughters unprotected into the wilds of perverse society to be chased like dogs in heat. And if we do, at least we have one deep consolation: our modern enlightened society firmly insists that all molested girls duly report every unwelcome advance to the proper authorities who will gamely prosecute the offenders to fullest extent of the latest date-rape laws. And that, if our daughters do not mind suffering the mild indignity of rape in the meantime, is the perfect solution.

On the other hand, for those of us who are somewhat troubled by the thought of our daughters being mauled by testosterone crazed maniacs (or, boy-iacs?), we could humble ourselves before the Word of God and search carefully for biblical guidelines instructing the man who pursues a wife. For starters we should reconsider the biblical basis for the authority of the father (and mother) over the bride-to-be. The Word of God makes it clear that kingdom authority flows through "headship." Paul asserted in I Corinthians 11 that authority flows downward through God→Christ→Man→Woman. Throughout the Word of God daughters are protected under their father's authority until they are given in marriage. Indeed, even the biblical language "given in marriage" reveals God's perspective on courtship: men "marry;" women are "given in marriage."

Under the Law, the father was his daughter's chaperone and the guarantor of her chastity. If a man married a woman and it was proved that she had been unchaste prior to marriage, then she was carried back to her father's house and stoned to death on the father's front porch (Deuteronomy 22:21). The father was responsible to guarantee a pure linage for the prospective husband by guarding his daughter's virginity. Also, if a young man defiled a daughter's purity before she was betrothed, the father had the prerogative to either require or forbid the man to marry his daughter (Exodus 22:17). Furthermore, the man was required to pay the father reparation. In each case, the father had the final say. Though we do not follow the code of the Law in every particular, we do believe that the Law is a shadow of God's will for us in the New Covenant. Thus, the principle of paternal authority is set forth for us to apply to our current situation. The world hoots and howls at this idea today, but while they are laughing themselves silly and wiping tears of mirth from their eyes, their daughters have slipped out the back window and become "Girls Gone Wild." Parents mock and children party. The sad thing is that the church has followed the world's lead and abandoned all biblical norms of parental authority, and we are shocked—yes, shocked we are!—to discover that our precious little girls are turning out just like the world. Someone, somewhere, sometime once said that you reap what you sow. He must have been a very wise man.

Of course, there is a great potential for abuse here, and we must be careful to balance the claim to parental authority with a responsibility to love and seek the best for our daughters. Just because the father has authority does not give him the right to abuse it. He should consult with his wife, and more importantly, with his daughter. No young lady should be forced into a marriage against her will. The Bible does not support the idea of arranged marriages as practiced in some heathen cultures. The story of Rebecca choosing to become the wife of Isaac stands as an example. Her family asked her what her desire was before they answered for her. Fathers must be careful to exercise their authority under the restraint and oversight of Scripture. Dad cannot rule as a brutal autocrat. He must humble himself before the Lord and seek to lead his family in faithful obedience to the Word of God.

Dad's authority must proceed from a self-sacrificing love that teaches his daughter what it means to be loved by a godly man. Girls are created to receive this sort of love, and by giving it, dad teaches her what to expect in a husband. This helps her discern the "thoughts and intents of the heart" when a young man comes calling. She can measure this newcomer against the outline of dad's ever-present shadow and determine whether he is a suitable suitor. Of course, when dad is properly involved, he will discern dimensions to the young man's character that the daughter cannot see. This sort of fatherly oversight shields the faithful daughter from unscrupulous predators who lust after her purity to defile it. In such cases, the wise daughter will not see her father's covering as oppressive, but as protective. The fence either holds you in or keeps the wild beasts out; it all depends on how you look at it. The Word of God teaches us that everyone in the kingdom of God is under authority, and Christian daughters are no exception.

But, as I was saying before that extended rant, the idea of "leaving and cleaving" requires the man to pursue, take and embrace a wife. The man takes the initiative and pursues— what we would call "courting—the young woman under her father's careful oversight. This means that the young man should leave his father and mother with the honorable intention of pursuing a wife in a godly way. He should taught to recognize the authority of the young woman's father. He should seek to be "authorized" by her father to court his daughter. This idea that a young man should seek the father's consent before paying his compliments to a young lady is not just a quaint old notion. It is a biblical notion, and we must preserve it.

Then, the young man must court the young lady under the oversight of her father in a family setting. He should spend time with her and her family. If the relationship develops, the couple should be allowed time together alone in a properly supervised setting. If a young man has a problem spending time with a girl's family, then that should serve as a warning to her and her parents. Marriage does not end family ties; it expands them. Our world has promoted the disastrous idea of dating where young people are thrust out into the night to cultivate their individual (read: selfish) interest in *one* another. But this flies in this face of the reality they will experience as soon as they are married. When they are married they will be required to align their new household with an extended family. When a man marries a girl, he marries her family. If he cannot relate well to her family prior to marriage, what makes us think he will do okay afterwards? The modern innovation of dating does not prepare young couples for this sort of greater interaction. In fact, it hurts their chances of melding together properly. A new family grows out of the old one. This is why it is called the family tree. Each new family is a new shoot, a new branch, on the tree. If they cut themselves free from their roots, then they may very well wither and die.

Our world has promoted this "myth of independence" for young men and women, in which children are encouraged to leave home and go out "on their own" until they decide to settle down and choose a spouse for themselves all by themselves. The family has been kicked under the bed here, and the formation of new families has suffered dreadfully as a result. The Bible projects a scenario where the young man is commissioned by his father and mother to pursue a wife under the godly oversight of her father and family. We should not forsake the family to establish a family. Family-building should be done in a family setting.

Obviously, this is a best-case scenario, and not everyone will have this sort of entrance into married life. And successful homes can be and have been built without this sort of blessing. However, this is the biblical ideal, and we should seek to implement it when and where we can. Many times newly married couples do not "cleave" right because they did not "leave" right.

CHAPTER 7

When a man and woman are married, they are formed by God into a "one-flesh" relationship. As Jesus quoted, "and they twain shall be one flesh." Now, there are three ways that this one flesh relationship is manifest. First, the man and woman are made one flesh in a legal, covenantal union. This moment occurs at the wedding when they are pronounced husband and wife. At the altar, they enter into a covenant before God and many witnesses. This covenant is a binding legal contract between God and the married couple. This marriage contract is recognized as legally binding by their family, by the church and by the state. Once this contract, this covenant, is declared valid and signed by all responsible parties, the man and the woman are no longer regarded as mere individuals before the laws of God and man. They have become one. Their property is joined, their interests are joined, and their destinies are joined. At this point, ever going solo again becomes very complicated.

When a man and woman are married, they become one body, a new *corpus*, a matrimonial and familial corporation. This is very similar to the corporate body that is formed when two business partners form a company and incorporate with the state. We could say that marriage creates *The Marriage, Inc.* Now, this is a very important concept for married folks, if they want to succeed at building a godly home. When we understand marriage as a corporation where two individuals form one legal entity, then we are well on our way to seeing why we must surrender our selfish interests for the greater interests of the larger corporation. If I may say so again, this allows us to see the greater cause.

Those who are incorporated together for a larger purpose must learn to subordinate the interests of the individual to the interests of the group. This is a sort of "team-concept" that must prevail in marriage. The man and the woman must each lose themselves in the larger good of the family. This is how we lose our life and find it again as Jesus taught His disciples. The family is joined together as one body under the headship of the man; he is the captain of the team. There is a covenantal unity that prevails because they have been legally formed into one corporate entity.

Now, covenantal oneness is not just an abstract idea, just a neat way of expressing a hope that we can all work together, a "Can't we all just get along?" attitude. No, covenantal oneness is more than that. Being made one flesh is a very real, legal relationship before God, and this legal status affects each member of the team. Just ask the business partner whose company is penalized because another member of his management team was caught ripping off stockholders or failing to pay federal taxes. One man may have committed the crime, but the entire business suffers as a result. The other officers cannot claim exemption from corporate penalty because they did not do the deed. They were joined together with the one who did, and that is enough. The legal ties of incorporation are very real. The same is true of marriage. Ask the alimony disbursing ex-husband if marriage is a real, legally binding relationship. Ask him if it is all just pure idealism and empty platitudes. He will turn out his empty pockets and brokenly assure you that the relationship is real. He is tied to that woman in ways that even divorce cannot dissolve.

And yet, the nightmare of civil divorce is just the beginning. The unfaithful man shall awaken to face the ultimate judge of marriage relationships, the Creator of marriage, God Himself. The writer of Hebrews assures us, "Marriage is honorable in all and the bed undefiled: but whoremongers and adulterers God will judge" (Hebrews 13:4). The covenant of marriage is made before God. And right here is where many people misunderstand the nature of the marriage covenant: they assume falsely that marriage is simply a contract between two people. They think the covenant is merely between a man and woman. That is not correct. The covenant is made *by* man and woman, but not *between* man and woman. The covenant is made *by* man and woman *between* the couple and God. They join together in one covenant with God as witness and judge. God joins them together, as we shall see below.

Marriage is a binding legal contract between God and the married couple. God extends the charter of marriage and allows the man and woman to enter this holy state. In a sense, to carry the business metaphor a bit further, God owns the franchise of marriage and grants them the license to be married. Man and wife are franchisees. God grants them authority to form a household. Therefore, they must operate *The Marriage, Inc* under the guidelines of company policy. God owns the family; husband and wife are its managers and stewards. And so, they shall give an account for their stewardship of the home at the final judgment when every man's work shall be tried with fire.

This covenantal idea of marriage is explicit in Malachi 2. It is evident from the passage that God views marriage as a covenant, as a legally binding agreement:

> And this second thing you do. You cover the LORD's altar with tears, with weeping and groaning because he no longer regards the offering or accepts it with favor from your hand. But you say, "Why does he not?" Because the LORD was witness between you and the wife of your youth, to whom you have been faithless, though she is your companion and your wife by covenant. Did he not make them one, with a portion of the Spirit in their union? And what was the one God seeking? Godly offspring. So guard yourselves in your spirit, and let none of you be faithless to the wife of your youth. For the man who hates and divorces, says the LORD, the God of Israel, covers his garment with violence, says the LORD of hosts. So guard

yourselves in your spirit, and do not be faithless. (Malachi 2:13-16 ESV)

The Lord God labels divorce and remarriage here as treachery and infidelity. This passage shows that Jesus' teaching on divorce was not really an innovation. He was preaching the will of God as previously proclaimed by the prophet. And it also shows that the perfidy of the Pharisees was nothing new. The language of Malachi indicates that God was pressing a lawsuit against the men of Israel. They were indicted as adulterers before the Lord's judgment bar. They had broken the terms of their covenant before God, and God was the One prosecuting their faithlessness. "The Lord was witness between you and the wife of your youth." Things are not going to be easy for these men on Judgment Day. Marriage is a covenant between the couple and God, and divorce is a violation of God's covenant marriage law. All of this shows the importance of understanding the covenantal aspect of the one-flesh relationship.

Second, the man and woman are made one flesh in sexual union, the physical coupling of sexual intercourse, which is the most obvious sense of being made one flesh. The man and the woman are joined together in physical union as a biological consummation of the covenantal union. They are made one flesh physically. And yet, we must emphasize here that the act of marriage is much more than just a physical union of two bodies; it is also the union of two spirits, the spirit of the man and the woman. Remember, God created Adam from dust and then breathed His Spirit into the man and he became "a living soul." This means that man is much more than just a physical, biological creature. Man is a spiritual being. Therefore, sexual union has a spiritual aspect that cannot be discounted. Those who fail to see the "soul-dimension" of sexual union fail to appreciate the fullness of sexual experience. The man and woman are joined together as one spirit as well as one body. So, the one-flesh relationship of sexual union is incomplete apart from the perfect union of spirits. Sexual union that is reduced to a merely physical act is sex without soul.

This is why fornication is so profoundly dissatisfying. God created the man and woman to be joined together covenantally in both spirit and body for a lifetime. Indeed, the spirits of the adulterous man and woman are joined, if only briefly, when they are joined physically. Paul made this clear in I Corinthians 6 when he rebuked the men at Corinth for sleeping with temple prostitutes. The man who sleeps with a harlot becomes one flesh—body and spirit—with the harlot. However, because there is no enduring covenant, the relationship is temporary. This does not mean that the man who sleeps with a harlot is married to her, for then fornication would constitute marriage. But it does mean that he is one flesh with her for the moment.

This highlights that the married couple must seek to be joined together perfectly in spirit as well as body when they are joined together in sexual union. The failure to be joined together spiritually is the root of much division in the home. When men or women bring multiple partners into their bed through their imagination, or when fantasies and role playing are indulged, or other such aberrant sexual practices are permitted, they are committing adultery in a spiritual sense and creating disunion where union ought to be. Jesus made this clear when He taught that men who look upon another woman with lustful intent commit adultery in their heart. It is possible, then, to defile the marriage bed through the lusts of the mind. We must understand the spiritual unity that God seeks between the man and woman as they are joined together in one flesh. It is not enough to be joined in physical union; married couples must be joined in spiritual union as well.

The one-flesh relationship of covenantal union leads to the one-flesh relationship of sexual union. It is the covenant that authorizes the sexual union. Otherwise, it is fornication. One leads to the other, thus those who have sex apart from covenant are interrupting the flow of authority. Thus, the sexual union becomes a loving expression of the covenantal union. The married couple acts out physically what is true spiritually in a sort of marital sacrament of communion. They are made one flesh in sexual union.

Third, a man and woman become one flesh in their children. Their offspring are them, both of them made one. This means that the one-flesh relationship extends throughout our generations into an everlasting future. This is where the one-flesh relationship becomes more than just any one couple joining together to live happily ever after. They are living ever after, all right, and hopefully they shall live happily, but they are doing so in the future through the lives of their children more so than they ever will in their present situation. They are creating a legacy and heritage of Christian faithfulness that shall endure forever.

And this brings us back to the greater cause. God made Adam and Eve one flesh for the purpose of extending dominion throughout the earth in their children. As they would have daily trained their children to do the work of God, they would have been enlarging the presence of their one-flesh relationship. This is dominion through discipleship, and we follow this same principle today. We are given children as the outgrowth of our one-flesh relationship much as the branches grow out of a vine. The Psalmist used this image to describe the family of a godly man growing out into the earth with his children extending his dominion like luxuriant boughs growing over the garden wall.

> "Blessed is every one that feareth the LORD; that walketh in his ways. For thou shalt eat the labor of thine hands: happy shalt thou be, and it shall be well with thee. Thy wife shall be as a fruitful vine by the sides of thine house: thy children like olive plants round about thy table. Behold, that thus shall the man be blessed that feareth the LORD. The LORD shall bless thee out of Zion: and thou shalt see the good of Jerusalem all the days of thy life. Yea, thou shalt see thy children's children, and peace upon Israel" (Psalm 128:1-6).

It seems the family tree really is an apt metaphor.

Covenantal union leads to sexual union, and sexual union leads to children. This chain of oneness must not be broken. This is the process by which God fills the earth with believers along with the evangelization of pagan converts. Therefore, the final goal of marital union is children. The greater cause rests upon the promise of a godly seed. God intends to accomplish His work through the propagation of godly families. We must recover this biblical view of children. We have considered children in a selfish light for too long. Our world esteems self and devalues children until God's "reward" (many children—Psalm 127:3) becomes a punishment to minimize or avoid at all costs. Every enlightened modern couple wants their trophy children, their boy and their girl. But to go any further brings amused inquiries regarding whether the unfortunate parent of more than two children knows exactly what causes that sort of thing. Having children is a problem that needs to be fixed.

When children are devalued it sets in motion a reverse decline of the one-flesh relationship outlined in Jesus' teaching. When children are devalued, sex is devalued. And when sex is devalued, marriage itself is devalued. Divorce becomes a reasonable option because the greater cause of a godly seed is no longer a priority. This is exactly what has occurred in our modern culture. We have discovered effective ways to prevent the nuisance of potential pregnancy thereby allowing sex to become merely a form of selfish recreation. Of course, I am not saying that God does not intend for a man and wife to enjoy their love whether or not they are producing children. He does. The Christian man should be ravished with the wife of his youth (Proverbs 5:19). But I am saying that when the greater cause of children is removed altogether, sex becomes perverted. Furthermore, I am not implying that Scripture bans family planning. It does not. But the Word of the Lord does address the wicked attitude against children to which we have succumbed. Scripture promotes a profound appreciation for an everlasting destiny born and borne in our children. Our attitude toward children must change to reflect the attitude of Scripture.

Men who lose sight of the purpose of bringing up their children "in the nurture and admonition of the Lord" (Ephesians 6:4) and exchange purpose for pleasure in sexual desire will become profligate adulterers and whoremongers. The only thing that can keep a man true and faithful for a lifetime is a sense of purpose that disciplines and transforms his sexual drive into a passion for an eternal destiny. The man who joins together with one woman in a lasting one-flesh commitment for the multi-generational propagation of a godly seed harnesses the incredible power of his sexuality, the manpower that most closely resembles the *ex nihilo* creative power of God, and plows his garden, sows his seed and produces a crop of children that shall be fruitful and multiply throughout the earth. And this is not merely a crass metaphor. It is a glorious understanding rooted in the Word of God. Children are the ultimate purpose of the family. It is all about the future. Even those who cannot bear children should invest their life and time into the future by reaching out to children in some way. Adoption or fostering is a good place to start. Mentoring is another. But however we apply the principles, they must be applied. The Lord God made us to become one flesh in our children. What God hath joined together, let not man put asunder.

CHAPTER 8

fter Jesus quoted Adam stating that a man and his wife would be one flesh, He pounded the point a second time: "Wherefore they are no more twain, but one flesh." Jesus took care to make sure that we get the point: two individuals are joined together into one body. Further, Jesus insisted that we understand what happens in the joining: "What therefore *God* hath joined together, let not man put asunder" (emphasis mine). The one-flesh relationship is not formed by man's will alone. Men and women are not married just because they decide to hook up together. Jesus asserted that a one-flesh relationship is the direct result of divine action. This one-flesh union is more than just a civil, physical or biological union, much more than just two people deciding to join forces in life for sake of a pleasant journey through this vale of tears. Men and women are made one for a greater cause than just a pragmatic arrangement of convenience. Jesus insisted that God joins men and women together in Holy Matrimony. God does it. And if God does it, then He does it for a reason—for a greater cause.

This changes everything. If marriage is a union formed by man, for man and through man, then man is the author of it and controls it according to his wish and whim. Of course, this is exactly how unbelievers (wrongly) see it. But if God is involved in the transaction, then it is quite possible that God will want to have some say in how things turn out. It seems likely.

Remember the larger context: the Pharisees came to Jesus asking if they could divorce their wife and get them another one for just any old reason that may strike their fancy. They were actually asking a question about their husbandly rights, about their total supremacy over women. They wanted to know if divorce was acceptable for every cause. Jesus replied with a firm, "No!" And this is the basis of His denial of their right to cast the woman out on her ear: God joined them together, and the man does not have the right to pull the marriage apart.

That was a rather radical idea, at least to those who did not understand the law and prophets. The Pharisees had read Malachi 2 just as Jesus had, but they missed the larger point. They missed the part about God's desire for a godly seed being greater than a man's desire to trade in his wife every three or four years for a later model. So, if Jesus could get them to see that marriage is God's initiative, not man's, then maybe they could grasp the larger point about the greater cause. God joins men and women together, thus only God can sunder their union.

Now there is something here that I would like to get a better grip on, something that has flickered around the edges of my mind for some time. Most of the time when we discuss this passage of scripture we focus on the Lord's warning concerning unlawful divorce, "Wherefore what God hath joined together, *let not man put asunder.*" And this is usually where the bulk of the discussion is directed on whether or not divorce is allowable under any circumstances. But as we rush to the more controversial topic of divorce we often blow right past an incredible affirmation of the sanctity of marriage: *God* joins men and women together. This means God does something in the wedding. The Almighty stands at the altar with bride and groom and sanctifies their vows before Him. Quite literally, God performs the marriage. The preacher is simply His representative.

Now this is a powerful idea. Too often we see marriage as a union formed by the will of two individuals and merely acknowledged by the church and state. And this is one of the fundamental reasons marriage is so disposable in our world today. If man (read: human) forms the union, then man may dissolve it at will. Furthermore, if man is the source and author of the union, then the union is only as strong as the two people holding it together. If the marriage is simply the union of two individuals who express a lingering sort of fondness for one another, then the only thing holding the marriage together is that fondness, and that can disappear rather quickly in our self-centered world. A marriage built on mere affection is built on shifting sand. However, if God is involved in the wedding, then we have someone to look to above and beyond ourselves for hope that the marriage may endure.

This leads me to consider again the idea of marriage as a covenant. God created marriage as a covenant between Him and the couple whom He marries. When the couple enters into covenant before God, the Lord pours out the grace of marriage upon them as they stand before Him. He pronounces them man and wife and joins them together in Holy Matrimony. God makes them one. This means *something actually happens* in the wedding that is spiritual and unseen. God "honors" the marriage (Hebrews 13:4) and "they are no more twain but one flesh." God does this.

This means God is present at the wedding as more than just the gracious provider of the gentle glow of sanctimony. God, the Creator of all things, is at work again forming a new creation, a one-flesh relationship that becomes the genesis of an enduring Christian heritage. The Creator gathers together the divided souls of the man and the woman He has formed from dust and gently, spiritually unites them together in a legal, covenantal union. After the wedding is over, the newly married couple will consummate their union in the presence of God and in the glory of the marriage bed, and God will join them together in physical union. Later, the Spirit of the Creator God will hover over their bed to bless them with children, and He will perpetuate their everlasting oneness through their children. But now, already, in this instant, at the marriage altar, they are one. God has made it so.

As I seem to say every other paragraph, this changes everything. But the reason I am saying this so often is because it is true. It does change everything. When we see our marriage as being formed by God rather than man, then we are able to place our trust in God for the preservation of the marriage rather than ourselves. We are able to place our faith in the grace of God that was given at the wedding when God made us one. And that is the key: when God makes us one, He provides the grace in the joining to keep us one. That is the point that I am trying here to grab with both hands. God gives grace in the joining, and the only way the union can fail is if we turn away in unbelief from what God promised in the wedding. God promised to make us one flesh, and He meant exactly what He said. The question is do we believe Him? When troubles arise and we are tempted to say with so many others before us, that we must not have been "meant for each other," when we are tempted to question whether we have enough in common to stay together, we can look back to this moment and recall what God did in our marriage. He made us one! God did it, not man. And that really does change everything.

Paul spoke in Ephesians (and elsewhere) about how God joins the body of Christ together by His grace. He said that "every joint supplieth" the nourishment that flows to the body. This is a powerful idea that shows how God supplies nourishment to the body through the joints, through the points where diversity is formed into unity. God is glorified in the joining, when disparate parts, each one bringing its own unique gifts and blessings, are joined together in one united purpose. And it is through these points of difference that nourishment flows. Just so, when God joins a couple together, their marriage shall be nourished through the joining, at the juncture of their individuality. In other words, as we discussed above, it is the areas where we are most different, and thus, we think, most divided, that we have the greatest potential for nourishment and strength. Of course, our response to the promise of God and to the reality of our joining will make the joint either our greatest strength or our greatest weakness.

As a pastor I am occasionally faced with couples who are ready to give up on their relationship. They will generally say something like, "We are just not sure we were really meant for each other." They mean that their marriage is out of joint. But their problem here is that they see themselves as the power that joins them. They are considering their own determination, their own power to make a relationship endure. They remember the promise they made to one another, and they are certain that they tried their best but their promise has failed. Now they do not seem to have the will to last another day. They feel certain it is time for the promise to be revoked, for the vow to be broken. Sadly, they are forgetting the most powerful part of the wedding as they look to the power of their word, to the strength of their promise to one another. They are overlooking the power of God's Word to them. It is my task as a pastor to remind them of what God did in the wedding. Somehow they must turn their eyes away from their own promise to one another and toward the promise that God made when He married them so long ago. They must place their faith in God's promise that He has joined them together as one. And if He made them one, then He has provided the grace for their oneness to endure. What God has joined together, let not man put asunder.

I have three questions for those who come into my office to announce their plans for a divorce. First, are you married? The answer to this one is generally pretty easy. A no-brainer, in fact. The unmarried do not enter clamoring loudly for divorce. Second, who married you? Now this one is a little more difficult. Most look a little puzzled and reply with the name of the preacher who officiated at their wedding. This is where the learning—or better, the *un*learning—begins. This is where I bring them to this scripture where Jesus solemnly intoned that it is God who joins men and women together in holy matrimony, which is the basis for our lack of authority to dissolve the union. I tell the divided couple that they must ask the Lord if they have permission to put asunder what He has joined together. And before they ask Him to authorize their parting of ways, we must ask the third question: If God joined you together is He able to give you the grace to keep it together? In other words, do God's joints fit? He is the healer of broken bones, as David reminded us in Psalm 51, and we must surely agree that when God joins something together, it fits. When the Creator makes a new world, it is good, very good. Thus, to pursue divorce would be to insist that God's work in making one out of twain has failed in this instance. Divorce is a mockery of God's promise at the altar. Do not put asunder what God has joined together. This makes divorce somewhat difficult to pursue conscientiously.

Marriage is a covenant. God enters into contract with the couple. God promises the couple that He will preserve them as one flesh, in each of the senses outlined above, and the couple promises God that they will persevere in the oneness He has created for the greater cause of a godly seed. God promises to take two individuals, no matter how different they may be, and form them into one body—if they will allow the grace of God to take effect. Obviously, the promises of God only work through faith. The couple must understand what happened when they were married and place their trust in God's promise to make them one. (Marriages, like souls, are saved by grace through faith.) Otherwise, they will see only their differences and despair of any chance to become one. This is how the beauty of true diversity is distorted into irreconcilable differences. Such people lose sight of the One who makes one out of twain. Divorce is a matter of unbelief.

In a biblical marriage the couple looks to the Lord to make two hearts one. Thus the focus remains on God. Unbelievers, however, look to themselves and attempt to merge individual self-interests into a common, mutual interest. Then, their marriage is built on the shaky ground of mutual interest, which can become un-mutual very quick. Then, the only mutuality they share is a mutual desire for divorce.

People in the world generally marry on the basis of what they call "compatibility." If they are compatible, as they define it, then they hook up, get married and stay together as long as they remain compatible. But when the gods of compatibility get restless, then the relationship must be sacrificed to appease them. And how is this compatibility determined? By studying self. The focus is turned inward to see what self needs—or merely prefers—and one sets out to find someone who meets this self-referential criteria. This is marriage by the "me" standard. This is marriage for the cause of personal happiness rather than the greater cause of seeking a godly seed. And if unbelievers marry for *compatibility*, then believers must marry for *covenant-ability* (to create a word out of thin air). The world believes that it is their mutual interests and common personality traits that will preserve the union; but Christians believe that it is the Word and Spirit of God that preserves men and women together in Holy Matrimony. The world looks to the power of compatibility; the church looks to the power of covenant. That is a fundamental difference, and once more, it really does make all the difference in the world.

There are a few more points to note in passing before we move further along in the text. First of all, when divorce occurs, it is man putting asunder what God joined together. Divorce happens when fallen man gains control of the home, when the family lives in the flesh. If we sow to the flesh, we shall always reap corruption. As Christians we must learn to pursue life in the Spirit in our homes. It is so easy to develop a dichotomy of Christian life where we live spiritually at church and carnally at home. But we must bring church home with us. We must make our homes a center of Christian faith. This can only be done through daily devotions, through regular family prayer, Bible study and worship. As the old saying goes, the family that prays together stays together. There really is a lot of truth in that.

Second, divorce does not always happen at the courthouse where lawyers and judges do the dirty work of ripping out the seams of what God sewed together. Sometimes divorce is a "virtual divorce" where a couple still sleeps in the same bed, eats at the same table, sits on the same couch, walks the same halls, drives in the same car, attends the same church, on and on, and yet they are divided in their hearts from one another. They are divorced in spirit if not in flesh. This tells us that we need to take heed to the teaching of Jesus on divorce even if we have never been to see the lawyer. There are more troubled marriages around us than those that sit on a counselor's couch. We can very easily be divided in our hearts and our homes while remaining together for a lifetime. We need more than apparent unity; we need real unity where the greater cause of the kingdom of God is diligently pursued in our everyday lives.

Third, we have seen above that the one-flesh unity of a marriage is formed in three successive stages: covenantally, sexually and biologically (in our children). If we are made one flesh in this order, then this is exactly how we are divorced. Those who drift apart into virtual divorce on their way to actual divorce do so in the realm of childrearing, love-making and then finally in the legal sundering of their vows. If a man and a woman remain united in the greater cause of childrearing and in their love-making, then they will never need to worry about a legal divorce. Divorce is simply the official recognition of what has already happened long ago.

Finally, divorce pits man against God. It puts man in the place of asserting that his reasons for putting asunder are greater than God's reasons for joining together. But God always wins this sort of argument. God is not impressed with all of our reasons for divorce. With rare exceptions, our reasons for divorce are nothing more than excuses for an unforgiving heart. If we forgive one another our trespasses, then divorce in never an option. Of course, forgiveness is based upon repentance, and reconciliation is a two-way street. Both parties to a marriage have to be willing to work it out, and there are exceptions that permit us to pursue divorce as a last resort when all attempts at reconciliation have failed, as Jesus explained later on. But the exception proves the rule. And regardless of the possible exceptions, this does mean rather emphatically that divorce *for every cause* is not recognized by God. When God joins a couple together, He means for it to last.

CHAPTER 9

The Pharisees were seemingly disconcerted by Jesus' response to their question. They probably expected nuanced considerations and extended discussions of all the causes that made divorce permissible. However, Jesus set up all of man's causes for divorce and smashed them into oblivion with the one greater cause, the cause of God. Jesus made the causes of man look petty in comparison, and He left no wiggle room for excuses. So, by the next verse, the Pharisees were standing on their tiptoes clamoring loudly for explanations. Fallen man cannot keep from talking back. He cannot accept the Word of God without demanding that God explain Himself. And look at what the Pharisees said: "Why did Moses then command to give a writing of divorcement, and to put her away?" The question opened then just as it does today: *Why?* Man has been asking God "why" ever since the garden when the serpent persuaded the woman to question the motives of God. And there is no subject where the "whys" fly thicker and faster than the subject of divorce. Just ask any pastor who has ever dealt with it. The situations and justifications pile up like autumn leaves blowing in the wind.

It is obvious that the Pharisees understood very clearly that Jesus was flatly condemning divorce. At that point Jesus had made no exceptions whatsoever (that comes later). And they were incredulous. So then, they asked, what about the Law of Moses and the commandment to issue a divorced woman a bill, a certificate, of divorcement? Jesus responded by acknowledging that Moses allowed divorce, but notice how He changed the emphasis: the Pharisees spoke of Moses' "command" but Jesus spoke of what Moses "suffered." Jesus made it clear that Moses' ordinance was not a divine institution or endorsement of divorce but rather an allowance regulating an existing practice. God did not ban divorce outright under the law (which shows it is not an unpardonable sin), but He did regulate it for the sake of the women who were victimized by it. And Jesus went on to say that Moses permitted this because of the hardness of their hearts. In other words, God allowed the men to put away their wives and give them a certificate of divorce as a show of mercy to the women. The hardness of men's hearts made divorce the only remedy available to rejected women. And Moses demanded that the cast-away women be given a certificate proving they were divorced and free to be another man's wife. Otherwise, the women could have been cast into the streets to die, or possibly even stoned as adulteresses if the moral taint was not removed by the certificate of divorce. Thus, the man was commanded to write out a bill of divorce for the woman's sake.

The Pharisees attempted to use Moses' law to justify themselves, but Jesus turned the law upon them to condemn them further. Jesus twisted their loophole into a noose. The very law they had used to justify divorce for every cause revealed and condemned their hardness of heart. "From the beginning it was not so!" Jesus cries. God never intended this, and if He had not shown mercy to the poor women left without recourse, divorce would have never been tolerated. The men are left with no excuses. God hates divorce!

And then Jesus took it even one step further. Not only has divorce for every cause been unacceptable to God from the beginning, but whoever divorces his wife for any old cause and "shall marry another, committeth adultery: and whoso marrieth her which is put away doth commit adultery." The noose was getting tighter. If the Pharisees had been incredulous before, they became absolutely speechless. At least, there is no indication that they had anything further to say. Not only is divorce for any cause disallowed, remarriage after illegitimate divorce is adultery, and adultery is punishable by death. No wonder Jesus' disciples, standing by listening intently, then piped up and said: "If the case of the man be so with his wife, it is not good to marry." Jesus' doctrine was radical and unprecedented, at least according to their traditional interpretation of the law of God.

Now, it is certainly true that Jesus did make an exception there in the middle of His discourse ("except it be for fornication"). But the point to be made now is that Jesus condemned divorce so vehemently that even the disciples were blown away by His doctrine. Something must have been really unusual about what Jesus was saying.

Even there Jesus did not back off an inch. The disciples seemingly could not accept what Jesus said. It would be better just to remain single, they said in stunned protest. Jesus turned abruptly toward them and said, "All men cannot receive this saying, save they to whom it is given. For there are some eunuchs, which were so born from their mother's womb: and there are some eunuchs, which were made eunuchs of men: and there be eunuchs, which have made themselves eunuchs for the kingdom of heaven's sake. He that is able to receive it, let him receive it." It would be better to remain celibate for the kingdom's sake than to trespass against the will of God and commit adultery through an unbiblical divorce and remarriage. No doubt everyone cannot accept this doctrine. But take it or leave it—that was Jesus' steadfastly simple approach. And after that, no one said much else about it. Matter closed.

Now, this is difficult material. Already, as some are reading, loud protests are being registered and fierce complaints being lodged. "What about the exception clause?" I seem to hear someone say. And there is no doubt the exception is there. Jesus did say that divorce and remarriage is adultery except in the case of sexual infidelity. However, before we rush to address the legalities of the exception clause (which, sad to say, we shall afford scant attention here), we must hesitate on the threshold of self-justification lest we imitate the error of the Pharisees and seek legalistic loopholes to excuse an overly tolerant view of divorce. We may at times have a right to pursue divorce and remarriage. But we cannot allow this narrow right to define our broader attitude toward divorce. We must share God's antipathy toward it. Even if divorce becomes necessary and permissible, we must hate every minute of it.

Divorce is a result of hardness of heart. Jesus went to the root of the problem. He declared that Moses permitted men to divorce their wives because he knew the hardness of their unregenerate hearts. Hardness of heart is a biblical metaphor that describes a man's proud refusal to hear the Word of God and receive correction. This sort of man is no longer tender in the presence of the Lord. He will not be entreated. Appeals for tender-mercies fall on deaf ears. He becomes harsh and unforgiving. Indeed, he becomes the very embodiment of the man that Jesus condemned in Matthew 18 when He commanded the disciples to pursue humility and forgiveness.

Paul warned against hardness of heart when he taught Christian men, "Husbands love your wives; and be not bitter (harsh) against them" (Colossians 3:19). The only way a man can cast his wife out into the street with a bill of divorce in her hand is if he has become hardened in his heart against her. He will no longer humble himself down and forgive whatever perceived wrong she has done. His hardened heart says "enough is enough" and casts her out. Divorce cannot happen until someone hardens his heart.

Thus, we have come full circle back to where we began. Divorce is a matter of pride and unforgiveness. If we humble ourselves before one another and forgive one another our trespasses, then divorce is never an option. If we shall build our marriages upon the greater cause of seeking a godly seed, upon the greater cause of dominion through discipleship, then our hearts shall remain tender before God and man. The man who lives for the greater cause chooses daily to subordinate his will to the will of God. The man who keeps his will subject to the will of God cannot develop hardness of heart. This is the sort of man who will figure out a way to humble himself and forgive every trespass until the amazing grace of God flows through his parched world like a river overflowing its banks. The love of God will keep his heart soft and merciful. And the more he shows mercy, the more mercy is shown to him, and he is spared the cruel indignity of divorce.

CHAPTER 10

I
t is no coincidence that just as soon as the narrative left the controversy with the Pharisees it moved immediately to the scene where Jesus blessed the children. As noted above, this is a providential arrangement of material. We started out by forsaking the wilderness of pride and unforgiveness, and we end up here cultivating the fertile fields of generational blessing. This is the destiny of the faithful Christian family. It really is all about the children, about the enduring legacy of dominion through discipleship. Though the disciples were still missing the larger point and sought to forbid the children from crowding the Savior, Jesus insisted then as He still does now, "Suffer little children, and forbid them not, to come unto me: for of such is the kingdom of heaven." The kingdom of heaven and its advance in the earth is directly connected to the Lord's blessing upon the children. This echoes what we have discussed throughout this study so far: the greater cause is the godly seed. Matthew deliberately concluded Jesus' discussion about divorce with the blessing of the children to drive the point further home. We must not miss the point.

There is more to be said here, but I must bring this study to a close at some point. This final point is as good as any, I suppose. Matthew 19 ends with Jesus warning His disciples about the evils of covetousness and materialism. Materialism is one of the greatest enemies of the modern Christian family. So many eternal things are sacrificed for temporal things, for the pleasures and entertainments of life. We can learn much from Jesus' teaching in these final verses. The rich young ruler is us. We, too, have walked away sadly from eternal life in favor of earthly possessions. We must rethink our priorities.

Jesus promised that those who give up the things of this world to pursue the riches of heaven shall be rewarded with eternal life in the world to come and the blessings of this life here and now. God is not unwilling for us to have earthly possessions. He just demands that we put His kingdom first. Are we seeking first the kingdom with our family, with our marriage and our children? Are we living for the "greater cause"? If so, then we are promised that all of these things, the things that the Gentiles seek, will be added to us (Matthew 6:33). We must firmly settle it in our hearts that we shall live continually for the greater cause.